MOROCCO

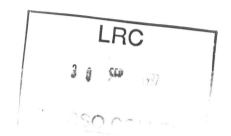

TIGER BOOKS INTERNATIONAL

Text
Nino Gorio

Graphic design
Anna Galliani

Map
Cristina Franco

Contents

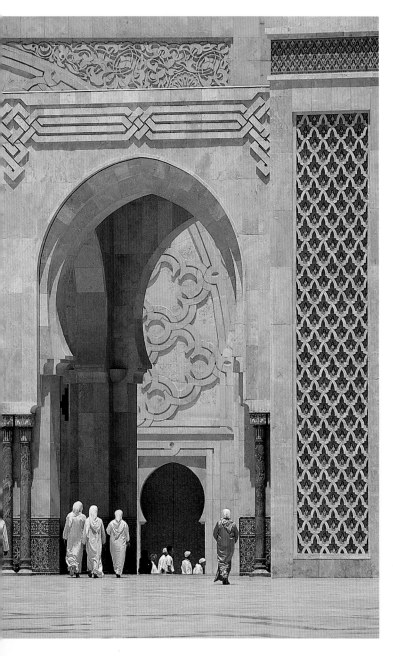

1 Kasbah *means citadel, fortress: southern Morocco has hundreds of them, with their high walls, tower houses, their rough "Desert of the Tartars" appearance. These buildings bring back memories of times not so distant when the southern flank of the sultans' Empire was exposed to the raids of the desert nomads. The kasbahs had to restrain the restless neighbours of the south, just as the Great Wall kept back the Mongols.*

2-3 *The Dadès river is one of the best known of the south: this is because it runs through the Valley "of a thousand kasbahs", which is full of fine fortresses; because it forms an impressive canyon (the Dadès Gorges); and because it marks an imaginary frontier beyond which lies the dry, harsh and intriguing air of the slowly approaching desert.*

4-5 *Chaouen is a piece of the Mediterranean transferred to the Rif mountains. Blue and white houses, neat roads, old Spanish dialect: what is a town like this doing in Morocco? It is there and it makes itself heard: it is indeed renowned for being a den of rebels. It all started with the arrival of some Muslim and Jewish refugees from Spain, a few centuries ago...*

6-7 *Ouarzazate is the first town encountered by those going beyond the High Atlas, the highest range in Morocco and marking the boundary between north and south. It has golf courses, gardens, good asphalt roads, but the kasbahs, like the one shown here at Taourirt, start just outside the town.*

8 *Casablanca is the largest city in Morocco, the third largest in North Africa. It is only natural that it should want the largest mosque in the country. Inaugurated in 1993, it bears the name of King Hassan II and rises from the sea with a minaret 650 feet high and huge doors.*

9 *Fez Jdid is one of the two old centres of Fez, the "moral capital" of Morocco. Its ring of walls also enclose a Royal Palace, one of the sovereign's secondary residences, its doors competing with those of the mosque in Casablanca. There are more royal palaces scattered around Morocco: at Méknès, Tetouan and Marrakesh, as well as that of Rabat, of course. The palace that stood in Tangier is now a museum.*

The Publisher would like to thank the Tourist Board of Morocco and the Royal Air Maroc.

This edition published in 1997 by TIGER BOOKS INTERNATIONAL PLC , 26a York Street Twickenham TW1 3LJ, England.

First published by Edizioni White Star. Title of the original edition: Marocco, i giardini di pietra dell'Africa. © World copyright 1996 by Edizioni White Star, Via Candido Sassone 22/24, 13100 Vercelli, Italy.

ISBN 1-85501-873-X

Printed in Singapore by Tien Wah Press. Color separations by Magenta Lithographic Con.

10 top left *Chaouen, in the Rif mountains, is characteristic for its blue and white houses, a clear mark of Andalusian architectural traditions.*

10 centre left *This solitary and austere kasbah stands in the Dadès valley. A few miles before the harsh, steep gorges that make it famous, the valley is wide, bright and green with small woods and well-irrigated fields.*

10 bottom left *The dunes of Merzouga rise suddenly at the edge of the Great Western Erg Dunes, fifteen miles or so from the border with Algeria.*

10 right *The coastline near Agadir, high, steep and rich in vegetation, overlooks the Atlantic Ocean.*

12-13 *Djemma el Fna is the best-known square in Marrakesh, indeed in all Morocco; it is a stage set in constant movement where acrobats and jugglers, story-tellers and vendors of knick-knacks perform. In the evening and by night it is even busier because the people tend to go out when the sun has set and the air is cooler. Winston Churchill was fond of this square, in fact he liked to stay in a hotel a short distance from it.*

14-15 *The walls of Marrakesh are among the most famous in the world: rising red amidst the palm groves they stir the imagination and dreams. Those who built them back in the Middle Ages had something else in mind. Marrakesh, the most fashionable city in modern Morocco, was born as a monastery-fortress for a sect of Islamic integralists.*

A T
O

DAKHLA

Introduction

An Arab legend says that the Earth used to be great garden: leafy palm trees, fragrant jasmines and sweet nightingales that filled the green land with their song. At that time men were all honest and sincere, so much so that the word "lie" did not even exist. Then someone told one: a small, insignificant one; but it was enough to ruin that marvel. Allah gathered all together: "Every time that you tell a lie," he said, "I will throw a grain of sand onto the world." The men shrugged their shoulders: "A grain? Who will see it?" No-one was concerned. Yet lie after lie, little by little the Sahara desert was formed: only here and there is there still the odd piece of that paradise that was, and this is because not all men tell lies. Who knows whether the inhabitants of Morocco are to be believed? According to the legend, some are, and some are not; their land is one third garden and one third desert: a sign that Allah has thrown down a good deal of sand, though not for everyone. As for the last third, that is all mountainous and should be considered neutral, because the story does not speak of it.

The Morocco of gardens is to the north-west: there are trees, vineyards and sumptuous towns. The desert stretches to the east and to the south, to the former Spanish Sahara, a still-disputed region, which in actual fact is not Morocco, or at least not for everyone. The mountains come last: to the extreme north is the Rif; then three central chains, very different from one other although their names are almost the same (Middle, High and Anti-Atlas).

Gardens, deserts and mountains are very different worlds. Only a trick of history could have compelled them under the same flag, that green star on a red background that flutters everywhere, almost obsessively, in the traffic-congested streets of Casablanca and on the summit of Toubkal, the roof of the High Atlas. But the bond between the three worlds ends there, as a glance at two places shows. The first is the Menara Garden in Marrakesh, where roses and cypress-trees stand at the edge of a delightful swimming pool, once a looking-glass for sultans and favourites. The other is the mouth of the Oued Drâa, a river that struggles for miles through imposing and desolate dunes before dying exhausted, suffocated by the sand, a hundred yards from the edge of the Atlantic Ocean. What do the refined Menara and the untamed mouth of the Drâa have in common? Nothing. Yet between these two extremes lies Morocco, land of flowers and sand, of storks and camels, of motorways and "blue people".

It is the most Western of the Arab countries, and 13 centuries ago, it was called by the armies of Islam Maghreb, the "land where the sun dies". The name has remained, albeit in joint-ownership with Algeria and Tunisia. Today, with the ports and road junctions of southern Europe thronging with North African dockers and car-windscreen washers, "Maghrebian" has almost become synonymous with immigrant; originally, however, that name stirred very different images: Maghreb evoked a distant, different, unreal land; a land that was exotic not only for the peoples of Europe. There where the sun dies, for centuries flourished a highly unusual civilization: Arab, admittedly, but only up to a certain point, for the inhabitants of the Maghreb were still above all Berbers, sons of the oldest native peoples of North Africa. Hence Morocco is a separate story in the Muslim world; for this reason it has nearly always been a sovereign empire, detached from the caliphs of the East. The forefathers of the emigrants who today in Italy and Spain sell cigarette-lighters at road junctions, once ruled a vast portion of the world, from Spain to Senegal.

This is, however, easier to believe after having visited the four "imperial cities", their courts and their treasures. There for centuries (from 786 to 1907) reigned six dynasties of sultans: the Idrissids, Almoravids, Almohads, Merinids, Saadians and Alawites. The Morocco of gardens and sultans can start only from Marrakesh, the best-loved and much-sung imperial city. We consider it first, perhaps for the red walls that rise from a large palm-grove, like an unexpected miracle; or because it stands against the backdrop of the unreal snows of the High Atlas, the gateway to the Sahara; or perhaps simply because it successfully guessed just what the jet set wanted: minarets and luxury hotels, *souqs* and golf courses. Whatever the reason, many have been seduced: writers, film directors, numerous VIPs. The first was Winston Churchill; then came Paul Bowles (*The Sheltering Sky*) and Gabriele Salvatores (*Marrakesh Express*); then Alain Delon, who bought a piece of palm-grove outside the city. Sweet and spoilt, worldly and dreamy: this is Marrakesh today. However, the city was founded with a very different purpose: it was born as the austere fortress of a religious sultan of the Sahara. One day, armed with his sword, the Koran and a few orange seeds, he went north in search of souls and land. His name was Youssef bin Tachfin, a charismatic leader of people; his army was not made up of Arabs but of Berber nomads and black Sudanese, which all Europe called Moors. It was the year 1070: Islam gained followers as far away as Spain; the nomads had fields, Europe discovered citrus fruit; and Youssef returned, bringing with him a lovely Andalusian girl as a prize, the future mother of all the Almoravids.

16 *Place Hassan II is the ideal centre of Tetouan, the most Spanish town of the Maghreb. The white houses, the Andalusian cuisine, the mixed languages are the legacy left by the colonial era: from 1912 to 1956 Tetouan was the capital of Spanish Morocco. Until 40 years ago the Sultan had only an ambassador here as if in a foreign country. Strangely, the headquarters of colonial Spain were right here in this very square, now named after the present King.*

17 top *Almost as if for revenge or to reassert sovereignty, the former capital of the Spanish colony is now one of the King's secondary residences. The Royal Palace of Tetouan overlooks the Medina and, in keeping with local architecture, avoids the luxury and arabesques of the other palaces, and merely displays blinding white walls.*

17 bottom *Despite the Spanish-like atmosphere, Tetouan still has a medina - the old town- whiter than white of course. Impressions apart, these alleyways appear typically Arab to the eyes. Roaming through this labyrinth you understand the true meaning of the name given to this town, which in Arabic means, more or less, "keep your eyes open".*

Mosques, souqs, the minaret of Koutoubia: Marrakesh reeks atmosphere. The best place of all is a square, Djemma el Fna, where every day the multicoloured fantasy of the Magreb is re-enacted: it is populated by story-tellers and fire-eaters, jugglers and magicians, snake-charmers and water-sellers. Youssef had nothing to do with all this: that playful and vibrant atmosphere is rather a revival of the soul of Ahmed al-Mansour, the sultan of another dynasty, the Saadians. It was he, in 1500, who made Marrakesh a temple of fine living, rich not only in walls and mosques, but also in secular art, flowers, games, odalisques, good food: a city of narrow streets fragrant with spices and pleasures, become exemplary and now synonymous with all Morocco.

Many traces of that refined and pleasure-loving Saadian world remain in the cuisine, and not only in Marrakesh: Moroccan cuisine is the best of the Arab world, on a par with that of the Lebanon. Amongst the most famous dishes is couscous (steamed semolina served with vegetables or meat) - now familiar to Europeans and found all over North Africa. More typically Moroccan are the *tajine* (chicken or mutton stew with vegetables, prunes and dates) and *bstilla* (an elaborate pie filled with pigeon meat, sugar, almonds, saffron and coriander): their balanced sweet and sour flavour is to a certain extent a reflection of the country, where sugar plays an important role and not just at table.

But is Morocco really all like this? If you climb up to the hills, you will discover the grim face of the Maghreb. It is called Méknès and it is the second imperial city; from afar it looks like a long snake, because it is encircled by walls, 25 kilometres of them. A titanic effort: one wonders how many worked at it. Méknès is the work of one Sultan alone, Moulay Ismail (1672-1727), of the Alawite dynasty. He sacked the ancient Roman city of Volubilis for the stones; to finance the works he legalized piracy; then to celebrate the work he beheaded on the bastions 700 "enemies" who had opposed the project. It is hard not to remember this as you pass through the Bab el Mansour gateway, all tiled with green majolica. Inside, a second circle protects Dar Kebira, the royal citadel: Ismail lived there, with a Pharaonic court said to have included 500 concubines, 12,000 horses, 25,000 slaves and 30,000 black militia. Huge stables are still there to prove that he certainly kept all those horses. The rest should be taken with a pinch of salt since the excesses of the lord of Méknès were used as propaganda by Europe, seeking an alibi for its colonial aspirations. Many have played at depicting Ismail as an Arab Dracula: from John Windus, an Englishman of the 1700s, who called him "a man the colour of death" to Michèle Mercier, sex-symbol of the Sixties, who dedicated a successful film in the series *Angelica* to him.

But Méknès - and hence Moulay Ismail - must be given credit for at least one thing: the hills outside the city produce the best grapes in the country. This is the Morocco of green leaves and flowers after all. The local wines are called Sidi Larbi, Gheromane, Sidi Bouhai: of course the Grand Cru de Bourgogne is a very different matter; but the reds, whites and rosés seem a miracle if you consider that the desert is not far away and that Islam forbids its followers to drink alcohol. Yet the grapes and wine are not produced in infidel, marginal areas: this is the heart of Morocco: a little north is Moulay Idriss, a holy city for Islam, where still today non-Muslims cannot stay overnight; and if you follow the vineyards you will come to Fez, the "moral capital" of the country.

Fez is the third imperial city: the oldest but above all the most real and the most learned. Most real because it has never put on a face for the tourists: the souqs are still markets selling crafts not junk; the large Kairouyine Mosque is entered only for prayer; and the white or pearl-grey houses in the old quarters (Fez el Bali and Fez el Jdid) show themselves as time has made them without pretence, in the precious portals of sculpted cedarwood and in the falling plaster. Enter the Medina, the largest and most intricate old centre of the Maghreb: there, in streets so narrow that two donkeys can hardly pass, amidst abandoned rubbish and flowering courtyards, you are back in the Middle Ages. But Fez is also the learned face of Morocco. This is demonstrated by the many *medersa*, Koranic schools where whole generations have learnt the alphabet and other things. The prime example is the Kairouyine university: the oldest in the world, it dates from 859; it is known all over North Africa because it has formed the leaders of various countries; we too owe it something, because centuries ago it had a small but great idea that changed mathematics: the number zero.

Who takes the credit for a city such as this? The Idrissid dynasty, which founded it; the Merinids who enlarged it; but also the anonymous craftsmen of various peoples (Arabs, Berbers, Andalusians, Jews) who 1200 years ago founded here a prolific multi-ethnic community. Still today, Moroccan craftsmanship offers its best in Fez, the fruits of a world that elsewhere is disappearing. Every shop has its master (*mallem*), every district its specialization: Nejjarine is the carpenters' *souq* with their cedarwood furniture; Seffarine, the square of metalworkers and dyers, is overflowing with embossed copper and multicoloured hanks of wool hung out in the sun. On the edge of the Medina are the picturesque and famous tanneries; the smell is always tremendous down there, but those arriving are offered a fragrant twig of mint, to save their sense of smell; with that twig held to your nose you walk amid large pits of vegetable colour, where the leather is tanned and painted before being turned into bags, pouffes and belts. Fez truly has the best in craftsmanship; but for carpets is it bettered by Rabat, the fourth imperial city, former cove of pirates and today the country's capital.

18 top *Taroudannt rises inland from Agadir; it is commonly known as "little Marrakesh" because in many ways it brings its famous cousin to mind; its walls in particular, which completely encircle the town, compete with the mightiest towers ever seen south of the High Atlas.*

18 bottom *The Chella necropolis, surrounded by walls, stands in the modern urban development of Rabat. The original site of the Phoenician port town, it was then occupied by the Romans, Berbers and lastly the Arabs; in the 13th century it became the burial place of the sultans of the Merinid dynasty. Today the interior is occupied by the ruins of the tombs immersed in green gardens.*

19 top *El Jadida means "the New": the town was thus called sarcastically by the inhabitants of the interior when they saw the Portuguese, already masters of other bases on the Atlantic, erecting this one. That was in 1510. Today El Jadida is a lovely colonial town on the ocean, south-west of Casablanca.*

19 bottom *An enormous underground cistern, its roof supported by round arches and columns, lies beneath the houses of El Jadida. This too is the work of the Portuguese: the huge water reservoir was to serve in the event of a prolonged siege.*

They say that this is all thanks to a stork: one day, as it flew over the houses, it dropped a piece of carpet, picked up who knows where, from its mouth; a woman found it, saw its strange design, copied the idea and made a fortune, because no one wove in that way. What is true is that the carpets of Rabat and the area around it are different from all the others; and that there are storks everywhere in the city; they nest on towers and minarets, looking down on everything and everyone, including the royal palace. The design of the carpets was not their invention: it is of Turkish origin. But it is pleasing to end this gallop through the Morocco of the sultans believing in storks; and to end it in Rabat, on the coast of the Atlantic, amid the tree-lined avenues that crown the Oued Regreg, one of the country's few rivers.

Look closely at that river: see how slowly but surely it pours into the ocean, between the walls of a fortress to the left and the beach of Salé to the right. You will not see any more outlets like this in Morocco: the Drâa is a mere thousand kilometres farther south, but it seems like another planet. Down there, where the rivers die in the sand, there are no storks nor tree-lined avenues: only the odd nomad, a few cobras and the ruins of a French fort (Tafnidilt), born to guard the boundaries of the world. Then there is the second Morocco, where the horizon widens, life is more sparse and history is not marked by the exploits of sultans, but by slow-moving caravans of "blue people". For the package-tour brochures, the Moroccan Sahara starts at Ouarzazate, just over the High Atlas; but this is a choice of convenience, tailor-made for the buses. In actual fact, the Sahara starts farther on: at Zagora, where a sign says "52 days to Tombouctou by camel caravan"; or at Erfoud, and the northernmost dunes of the country; or at Goulimime, where the Saturday market draws hundreds of nomads in blue *chech* (headcloth). They are not *tuareg* but *r'guibat*; though they have the customs and pride of their more famous cousins.

It is a strange Sahara, that of Morocco: it has not the boundless distances filled with nothing that cover countries such as Algeria, Chad or Mauritania. The views are similar, it is true: sometimes animated by dunes (*erg*), often stretching out in stony, moon-like plains (*hammada*). But here oases often appear amid sand and stone and they are frequently reached on good asphalt roads. The symbol of this Sahara, arid but not extreme, burning but with intervals of shade, is the date palm; according to a local saying this plant "grows with its head in the fire but its feet in the water". Date palms are to be found in all the oases, but especially at Tafilalt, the region around Erfoud, which has almost 7,000. In many ways, however, this part of Morocco has much in common with the rest of the Sahara: language, for instance (the *r'guibat* of Goulimime understand the Moors across the border far better than the Arabs of Casablanca), and religion (in the north the holy place par excellence is Moulay Idriss, but here Tamgrout is more important; it conserves ancient copies of the Koran, illuminated on gazelle hides). Also, the local hero is Ma el Ainine, theologian and warrior of the Sahara, who at the beginning of this century wrote 450 books and kept the French invaders on the run for nine years. Lastly, typical of the Sahara is the mentality of the people, who consider the desert one country and the frontiers simply a bizarre theory found in atlases, with no true correspondence to reality. That the frontiers are optional is after all demonstrated by the matter of the former Spanish Sahara, the region that borders the Atlantic, south of the Drâa valley as far as Mauritania. Invaded in 1976 by a "Green March" of Moroccan civilians, then occupied by regular troops, that sea of sand was the scene of a bitter war with the local independence-fighters of the Polisario Front. The conflict ended in 1988 with the promise to entrust the future to a referendum. Rabat has actually occupied the region, which brought with it the phosphate deposits at Bou Craa, one of the richest in the world. The referendum has still not happened.

From sand to snow is not such a long step: just 249 miles, the distance between the mouth of the Drâa and Tizi n-Test, the highest pass in Morocco (6,890 feet) on the High Atlas. And here is the third Morocco, that of the mountains: a not very African world which in spring turns all shades of green. Up there are orchards with almond and fig trees, forests of cedar and oak, even winter-sports resorts, with ski-lifts and ski runs: Ketama in the Rif Mountains, Oukaimeden in the High Atlas, Ifrane in the Middle Atlas. The last is the most unusual: a Swiss-style village where you sleep in unlikely Alpine chalets and ski in woods inhabited by monkeys. This too, like it or not,
is Morocco. Of course the traditional architecture of the Magreb mountains is different: the *kasbah*, the *ksour* and the *irhrem* scattered mainly in the valleys of the south. The *kasbah* are military forts, built by the ancient lords; the *ksour* (singular *ksar*) are villages enclosed in mud walls; lastly the *irhem* (or *agadir*) are fortified granaries still used to store crops, even though the risk of robbery is no longer a problem. The most famous area for this architecture is the Dadès valley, north-east of Ouarzazate, called the "valley of a thousand kasbahs". The most intact *ksour* are set amidst the pink granites of the Anti-Atlas, reached on dirtroads where only donkeys and four-wheel drive can pass.

Ksour and chalets, donkeys and ski-lifts: the Moroccan mountains are by no means all the same; nor could they be, stretching as they do from the Mediterranean to the Sahara. But they do have one thing in common: among the furrows and canyons of the mountains live communities of Berbers, descendants of the most ancient inhabitants of the Maghreb, who took the religion of the Arabs but often not the customs, nor the language, nor the designs of the rugs. They are

20 top *Mdiq is a small village on the Mediterranean coast popular with European tourists. Before being a holiday resort it was a holy place, as is demonstrated by these* koubba, *small sanctuaries dedicated to those who died in the odour of sanctity.*

20 bottom *On the Rif, not far from Chaouen, below Mount Tisouka, stands a mosque in the Spanish Moor style. It was built by the Muslim refugees, forced to leave Spain after it was "reconquered" by the Christians, who took refuge on these mountains: on a clear day the Spanish coast can be seen across the Strait of Gibraltar.*

21 *Gaudily dressed and always carrying bells to draw attention even in the thickest crowds, water or tea vendors are characteristic figures in the masses that fill the towns and cities of Morocco.*

22-23 *The Rif is a mountain chain running parallel to the Mediterranean for 200 miles, in parts green as only cedar woods*

can be. Inhabitants of these mountains are reluctant to accept external authority of any kind and rebelled first against the colonial troops, then against the Moroccan government. But the Berbers of the Rif are not famous for their long, anarchical resistance alone; they have a delightful town, Chaouen, where you would think you were in Andalusia.

24-25 *Of the towns on the Atlantic coast, Essaouira is the most fascinating; a former Portuguese naval base, it is the great historic rival of Agadir. It is surrounded by walls and still conserves the ancient cannons used by the Portuguese troops to control navigation along the Atlantic coast. Splendid, though not very well known, it is today the object of a learned and refined tourism.*

26-27 *The dunes of Merzouga are the first of the Great Western Erg (Dune), the vast expanse of sand that starts in Morocco and then plunges for hundreds of miles into Algeria.*

famous for their silver jewellery, for the coloured veils worn by the women, for their fanciful legends, and for their rugs, coarse to the touch, with diamond-shaped designs, whose colours differ from place to place: beige prevails in the Middle Atlas, red and ochre in the High Atlas; red-white-blue towards Ouarzazate.

"Berber" is really a general name, used all over North Africa to indicate different peoples: in Algeria it includes the Tuareg nomads and the peasants of Kabylie. The Moroccan Berbers descend from three lineages (Masmuda, Sahnadja and Zenata) and are split into many tribes, often called Beni ("sons of") plus the name of the family. The forefathers are many, as is shown by the variety of their features: in the Rif there are people with light-coloured eyes, on the Drâa others with dark skin. Sometimes the tribes recognize each other by their veils (if a woman wears a light-blue one she comes from the Oukka area; if it is black, she is from Dadès); others by a traditional skill: this is the case of the Souss Chleuh of Tafraoute, famous spice merchants. The Beni Hillal, on the other hand, are identified by the answer to a conundrum, or rather three answers: what is the lightest thing in the world? What burns most? What is the sweetest? Any Berber will say: a feather, pepper and honey. Only a Beni Hillal will give the right answer: the lightest thing is gunpowder in the barrel of a gun when you are facing the enemy; what burns most is the heart of a lover before his loved one; the sweetest is a tent full of children on the return from a journey. The triple truth is contained in a tribal legend: it tells of a certain Dyab who, thanks to these answers, was made sheikh. The elders of the village decided that "Despite his youth, he already knows everything about life". We could close here. But there is a fourth Morocco, not mentioned at the beginning: it has no gardens, nor deserts, nor mountains, but modern buildings and streets full of traffic, like Casablanca; or swimming pools and busy hotels, like Agadir; or queues of emigrants boarding ships to pursue a myth called Europe, as happens on the jetties of Tangier. It is modern Morocco, independent again 40 years after the colonial interlude. In this Morocco, Casablanca is no longer the magic and ambiguous city that lent its name to a famous film of the past starring Humphrey Bogart and Ingrid Bergman; it is a metropolis of three and a half million inhabitants, growing amid sequins and problems, just like all the large cities of the world. There is to be found the largest mosque in Morocco, named after Hassan II, the King who sits today on the throne that was of Youssef the Austere, Ahmed the Refined and Moulay the Surly. Inaugurated in 1993, it is one of the wonders of Islam: it cost 534 million dollars, can hold 100,000 worshippers and has a minaret 656 feet high, from which a laser points 22 miles towards Mecca. There, in Casablanca more than elsewhere, is at stake the future of a country thousands of years old, rich in glory, art and culture.

Mountains, oceans and deserts

28 top *Cap Rhir on the Atlantic Ocean to the north of Agadir is one of the westernmost headlands of Morocco. It is lapped by warm blue waters teeming with fish and, despite being well within reach of the busiest tourist resort on the Moroccan coasts, its beaches are far from crowded.*

28 bottom *The Rif near Ketama offers decidedly mountainous scenery, grassy ridges alternating with cedar forests. The Rif chain runs parallel to the Mediterranean for 200 miles in the north of Morocco. Ketama is one of the three main ski resorts in the country.*

29 *The Dadès valley is also called the "valley of a thousand kasbahs" for the profusion of fortifications present. It runs to the south of the High Atlas and offers predesert scenes, already stripped of vegetation and with all the shades of ochre: a foretaste of the Sahara proper. The* ksour, *the fortress-villages of southern Morocco, often have the same colours.*

From wave
to mountaintop

30 top left *On the coast to the south of Casablanca, just outside the city, at a place called Sidi Abderrahman, a scattering of white houses overlook the ocean set around a small koubba topped with a cupola.*

30 bottom left *Not far from Asilah, a seaside resort on the Atlantic near Tangier, the coast alternates sandy stretches and jagged rocks. This whole area is affected by currents and strong tides, making it difficult*

to moor; at the begining of this century it was still the stronghold of bandits.

30 right *Al-Hoceima is a small town born in 1926 as a Spanish military base and standing on a sheltered bay along a rugged stretch of the Mediterranean coastline.*

30-31 *Despite its long coastline, Morocco has never been a nation of navigators: as a result, although inland every step reveals traces of the native culture, the bays and capes tell the history of others, mainly the Portuguese and Spanish. Cap Rhir served for centuries as a landmark for Portuguese ships, the imaginary boundary between the regions controlled by Essaouira and Agadir. Once both cities were Portuguese naval bases, today they are both famous holiday resorts.*

32-33 *This mosque stands on the first spurs of the Rif but in sight of the Mediterranean; found a short distance from Ketama, in the extreme north of the country, it symbolically marks the passage from the blue Morocco of the sea to the green land of mountains.*

33 top *The mountains of Morocco are a precious water reservoir: often when crossing them you will encounter rivers, waterfalls and dams that form artificial basins. The most spectacular falls are perhaps those of Ouzoud on the Middle Atlas more than 300 feet high and supplied by the Oued el-Abid, a river which slightly lower down forms a number of interconnecting lakes.*

33 bottom *Water in plenty allows three out of four mountain chains (Rif, Middle and High Atlas) to give rise to spectacular forests, such as the cedarwoods around Ketama, in the heart of the Rif range.*

34-35 *This wall, created by nature, rises in a few miles from sea level to almost 8,000 feet: seen from afar the Rif always impressed the navigators sailing towards the Pillars of Hercules. On closer inspection it is still impressive but in a different way: the majestic peaks seen only as an outline become huge mounds where man has left his mark, tracing fields and villages on the slopes. Jealous of their mountains and ever rebellious, the inhabitants of the Rif speak their own language.*

33

36 top left *In spring, as soon as the snow melts, the Moroccan mountains burst into flower. Thanks to the latitude, which raises the temperature, and the frequent rainfalls caused by the Atlantic fronts, which guarantee irrigation, the High Atlas is a veritable glasshouse of wild species of trees. In Europe these live only slightly above sea level but here they reach far greater heights: one is this agave, flowering near Oukaimeden, at a height of 8,000 feet.*

36 top right *Man also benefits from the fertile mountains, sometimes performing miracles of patience and tenacity. These fields of maize are close to Taddert, on the High Atlas between Marrakesh and Ouarzazate, at a height of 3,000 feet. In order to grow them, the local inhabitants had to plough the stony ground of a small ravine, build dry walls and repeatedly repair them, put seriously to the test by the frequent summer floods of the not distant Oued Zate.*

36 bottom *Oukaimeden is a ski resort in winter, one of the most important in Morocco, but in spring its slopes are covered with flowers.*

37 *The Tizi n-Tichka (7,478 feet) connects Marrakesh to Ouarzazate and is the highest pass in the country. The road to it climbs steep, narrow hairpin bends in a charming but slightly brooding landscape. The scenery is softened only by the blossoming oleanders which accompany the road to the top. The Tizi n-Tichka, with its "twin" Tizi n-Test, has always been an important communication route between north and south Morocco. The descent towards the Sahara commences just beyond the pass.*

38-39 *Saying Oukaimeden in Morocco is like saying Cortina d'Ampezzo in Italy, Val d'Isère in France or Garmisch in Germany: it is the country's leading ski resort but only in winter of course. The Oukaimeden plateau is covered with snow from December to June, a chair lift climbs from the 8,692 feet of the village to 10,800 feet and is just fifty or so miles from a city like Marrakesh, rich and civilized enough to guarantee a constant flow of clients. In summer this Moroccan ski resort is transformed: the snow disappears, the ski runs become mountain meadows, the chair lift stops. This is the time to put on your climbing shoes and go trekking on the nearby mountain tops. Not Toubkal, the highest mountain in Morocco (13,661 feet) (though it is not far) but those smaller mountains around the giant: collectively they are known as Adrar n-Dern and are part of a national park, created to protect the landscape more than the fauna, not abundant here. Also of interest is a visit to the old Berber village, now abandoned, that gave its name to the modern winter sports resort.*

39 top *When the snow disappears a lovely mountain lake appears on the Oukaimeden plateau: then the scene is just like that of certain European mountains. It is surprising considering that Tizi n-Test , one of the passes leading to southern Morocco, is not far away and where the first dunes of the Sahara and the "blue people" are to be found.*

39 bottom *One of the greenest valleys of the High Atlas is that of the Oued Zate, a river which descends from the Tizi n-Tichka towards Marrakesh. Here pine trees, oaks and oleanders grow spontaneously and the Berbers grow maize and oats. Thanks to the fertility brought by the river, the valley is one of the most densely populated of the chain: the major villages include Taddert and Zerekten. This region, traditional fiefdom of the noble el Glaoui family of Marrakesh, is know as the "pays Glaoua".*

On the mountains of the frontier

40 top *Although the pictures in the holiday brochures depict Morocco as a hot country, snowfalls are not a rarity on the Middle Atlas mountains.*

40 bottom *The Berbers that live in the Anti-Atlas near Tafraout, all of the Chleuh tribe, build their houses with stone taken from the mountains, making their villages and towns perfectly camouflaged. This effect is even more striking in the winter months when the snow softens all harshness and blurs the perceptions.*

40-41 *An expanse of fields covered with a veil of snow, a small cluster of rural houses enveloped by the oppressive smoke of a chimney, the horizon closed by a chain of woody rises beneath a leaden sky: it could be a winter scene on the Italian Appennines or the Massif Central in France: instead it is a view of the Middle Atlas.*

42-43 *The Dadès river valley, in the south of the High Atlas, is known as that of "a thousand kasbahs" for the recurrent presence of noble and military castles, used by local sultans and emirs in the past centuries to strengthen the "frontier" of the Sahara, periodically crossed by nomad marauders. Around every kasbah, even where the river bed is dry, the vegetation is always lush, in striking contrast with the surrounding landscape which becomes increasingly ochre-coloured as you travel south.*

44 top left *On the southern side of the High Atlas, although the climate is hotter and drier than on the opposite side, the Berbers again have created well-tended fields, divided by dry walls. It is clear, however, that the mountains in the background are decidedly arid; the High Atlas itself is responsible for this as it blocks the Atlantic fronts; this means that rain is frequent north of the range but far less so to the south, with obvious consequences on the vegetation.*

44 bottom left *The Dadès Valley, as that of the Oued Zate farther north, was in part controlled by the powerful el Glaoui family. One of the "thousand kasbahs" of Dadès is still named after them. The el Glaouis had a palace of such luxury and majesty in Marrakesh that it is now the local residence of the present King, Hassan II.*

44 right *The road running from Ouarzazate into the Dadès valley is dotted with* ksour, *the fortified villages of the Berbers. For a long stretch, as far as Boumalne, the landscape is relatively gentle, partly thanks to the presence of crops and green walls of trees. Then the valley narrows suddenly in the Dadès Gorges, a sort of Moroccan version of the Grand Canyon. One of the most interesting of the ksour is El Kelâa of M'Gouna, specializing in the cultivation of roses.*

45 *Some of the Dadès kasbah are often used as sets for films with a desert flavour. This is the case of "The Sheltering Sky" and some time ago the "The Lion and the Wind". As well as the Dadès valley another area of interest for the* ksour *and* kasbahs, *but much less frequented by tourists, lies on the southern slopes of the Middle Atlas, in the Goulimime region.*

46-47 *Beyond the Boumalne* ksour *where the Dadès becomes embedded in the canyon, the valley suddenly becomes more barren. The thinning vegetation favours the erosion of the soil by atmospheric agents: rain and above all wind. The smallest particles torn from the rock will be carried far by the first spring storm and will, in the end, accumulate in large expanses that cover all else. This is how the desert is born and how it spreads. It has been calculated that in southern Morocco the sand spreads very slowly, just a few inches per year unlike other countries such as Niger or Mali where the Sahara advances at the pace of a few feet per year.*

A glance at the dunes

48-49 *The "thousand kasbahs" of the Dadès valley are, in a way, the Great Wall of the Sahara: the long row of citadels served to mark the boundary between the "civilised world" of the sultans and the lands of the nomads. Still today, the impending presence of the Sahara starts to be felt here. It is curious to note that most imperial dynasties of Morocco (Alawites, Almoravids, Almohads, Merinids and Saadians) originated south of the kasbah line.*

49 top *The Ifoultoute kasbah is not strictly speaking part of the Dadès valley. It stands just 6 miles from Ouarzazate, the end of the road that climbs over the High Atlas starting from Marrakesh. But the style is no different: very high walls and tower houses recur along the whole "defensive belt" that marked the southern boundary of the Morocco of the sultans.*

49 centre *The Sahel (i.e. the coast), as the strip that precedes the desert is called in Africa, is sometimes very green. This is so for the Tafilalt region where palm groves stretch as far as the eye can see. The date palm has always been the main source of nutrition for the peoples of the sub-Sahara; at Erfoud, the capital of Tafilalt, a celebration dedicated to this popular fruit is held once a year.*

49 bottom *Wind and rain erosion has fashioned this mountain to the south of the High Atlas, near Ouarzazate. The plain also bears the signs of erosion: it is formed of the heaviest debris that the atmospherical agents have detached from the mountain. The lighter detritus is carried farther away and with time will accumulate to form dunes.*

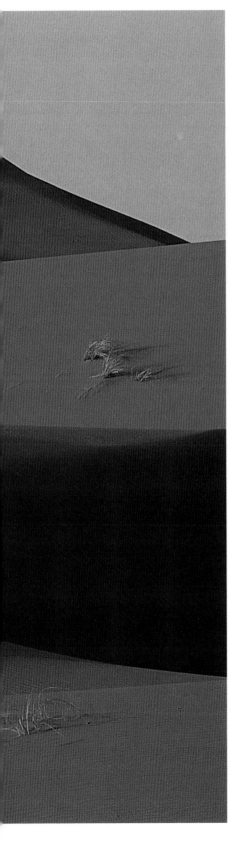

50-51 *At last: the first sand dunes rise at Merzouga, twenty miles or so from Erfoud, the capital of Tafilalt. Right on the border with Algeria, not far from a former French fort, these represent the outpost of the immense Great Western Erg, one of the largest expanses of sand in the world, which continues into Algerian territory for hundreds of miles.*

51 top *The dunes of Merzouga are yellowish in colour as is nearly all the Great Western Erg. Not all of the Sahara is so: much of the desert has decidedly more reddish hues. The colour of the dunes depends, of course, on their chemical composition, but the colour also varies according to the inclination of the slopes, thus according to the angle of incidence of the light.*

51 centre *According to an Arab legend, the dunes were formed by grains of sand thrown by Allah from the sky as punishment for telling lies. By the same legend, the Sahara will disappear the day that man becomes sincere once more. For the moment, the desert continues to advance. This can be seen close to the dunes of Merzouga, where the sand is gradually covering the asphalt road from Erfoud.*

51 bottom *Rissani is a tiny village in Tafilalt, south of the more important Erfoud. It is so small that no map would show it, were it not for two very special reasons. The first is that Rissani is the last inhabited village before the vast Sahara begins. The second is that this microscopic village was the cradle of the Alawites, the royal dynasty that has ruled for almost three hundred years, the present King Hassan II being the heir. Rissani erected a mausoleum to the founder of the family, Moulay Shereef, who lived in the 17th century. This was seriously damaged some years ago by a flood, strange as that may seem.*

Folklore and much more

52 top *Nearly all the most important celebrations of the year have a religious origin. One of the most heartfelt is Mouloud, which commemorates the birth of the prophet Mohammed and is held on changing dates (summer-autumn) as, like the Christian Easter, it is calculated on the basis of the lunar calendar. In towns and the most remote Berber villages alike the "Islamic Christmas" is celebrated with dancing and processions in costume.*

52 bottom *Religion pervades all aspects of life, eating and dress included. As in all the Islamic world, women cover their heads with a veil; the Moroccan version is called* l'tam *and is usually brightly coloured.*

53 *Unlike other Muslim countries, the women are not legally bound to wear a veil: it is merely suggested by tradition and a hint of vanity is always present. Berber women are indeed famous for the jewellery they flaunt with coquetry.*

54-55 *"Where the water starts, freedom ends" says a proverb of the Sahara. This instinctive suspicion of rivers and sea has not contaminated the inhabitants of northern Morocco, who live far from the Sahara. The Loukkos, a river that plunges down from the Rif chain into the Atlantic near Larache has always attracted the locals for the very abundance of its waters. The fishermen's boats have always been seen here. Numerous bathers have started to visit the river estuary: this is a new phenomenon, the sign of a rapid evolution of customs. The huge flow of tourists from Europe to which Morocco is accustomed is producing imitation, on the one hand opening Moroccan society to new prospects, but on the other risking its distortion.*

55 top *The beaches of the river Loukkos are a good indication of the changes coming about in the habits of the Moroccan people. Men are at ease in swimming trunks, until a few years ago considered unseemly. Women's dress has however changed little, even on the beach and "bathers" can often be seen wrapped in their* l'tam.

55 centre *The coastlines of the ocean, the "great desert of water" are also the object of a growing seaside tourism. One of the most crowded beaches is that between Casablanca and Rabat.*

55 bottom *The beach of Essaouira is popular among the Moroccans and the tourists alike. As a matter of fact, the well-equipped tourist villages so popular among the Europeans are only a short distance away.*

56-57 *The* l'tam *remains the most ingrained symbol of Moroccan traditional costume: normally made of woven cotton, the veil is hand-dyed in bright colours. The dyers' workshops, with rows of* l'tam *hanging out in the sun, supply a characteristic note of cheer in the medina.*

58 top left Medina *is an Arab word, used for the old town centre, the hub of Moroccan life and where shops, markets and craftsmen are amassed. The medina of Marrakesh is almost entirely occupied by a souq (market) selling, among other things, quality carpets.*

58 centre left *Commerce is one of the Moroccans': favourite activities; those who are not merchants full-time become occasional ones. This is so for the peasants who, after the fruit harvest, come to the city or to the weekly markets in the villages to sell their produce directly. Even the most central of squares, such as Djemma el Fna in Marrakesh, has temporary stalls such as this one. Bargaining is no longer the custom in the cities but is frequent at the village markets.*

58 bottom left *The houses of the medina are often transformed into popular picture galleries as the Moroccans love to adorn their homes with murals; this one is at Asilah.*

58 right *Among the most commonly-found workshops in the medina are those of the dyers who use vegetable colours. The best ones are in Marrakesh.*

59 *Tanners are characteristic of the medina of Fez; they produce coloured leather for bags and belts that are of excellent quality. Courtyards with large rows of basins stand amidst the mass of houses: each basin contains a different shade of dye and the leather is left to soak, sometimes for days on end.*

60-61 Sometimes the streets of the medina are so narrow that two donkeys can hardly pass and so full of goods on display that it is hard not to tread on something. This is true of Fez el Bali, the most ancient of the two old centres of Fez; it is the largest medina in the Maghreb, an intricate maze of narrow streets divided into smaller districts where one craft prevails. This means that there is a blacksmiths' district, one of potters, one of carpenters, one of goldsmiths.

61 top In Fez el Bali, the prototype of all the medinas in Morocco, an important part of the "street life" is played by the food sellers, especially vegetable traders. Eating is an important part of Moroccan culture and its cuisine is the best in the Arab world.

61 centre In Moroccan villages, sales are preceded by endless bargaining, at times enjoyable, at times exhausting. Bartering is not only used for luxury items but for everyday commodities such as dates and olives. As well as serving to set the right price for goods, finding a point of balance between demand and supply, bargaining often becomes an opportunity to socialize and exchange news and opinions. Until some years ago, before television, the market was where most news was passed on. Trying to avoid bartering, saying any old price and then immediately refusing, is seen by the counterpart as an impolite and unpleasant gesture, as if more importance were attributed to the object than the seller, with whom you do not wish to waste your time.

61 bottom The European traveller visiting Morocco for the first time tends to be drawn into the cheerful and clinging atmosphere that appears all over. Care is needed to avoid spending huge sums on souvenirs of no value, especially in the souqs where a great deal of trash circulates. In the souq of Fez, however, attractive craft objects such as those shown here, can be found, to suit all wallets.

62 top left *There is a time for strolling in Moroccan cities, usually late afternoon when the air is cooler. Almost as if to show that Arab women are not always kept in the home, they are often seen in groups out for a breath of fresh air. In fact, 70 per cent of the time, when women appear in public, they are not veiled.*

62 bottom left *The imaginary wall erected by the Moroccans to defend their privacy is comparable only to the impenetrable walls of Taroudannt.*

62 right *It is quite rare, at least far from the large cities, to see husband and wife strolling together. Whenever this happens the man usually precedes the woman by a few steps. This is local etiquette, now more and more outdated.*

63 *Religious precepts are ingrained in Moroccan culture and customs. This applies both to the remote villages in the Atlas and to the large cities. Even in Casablanca, a metropolis of European appearance, people stop at the time of prayer and turn ritually towards Mecca, bowing and kneeling repeatedly. This rite is particularly solemn on Fridays, the Muslim holy day. The faithful are called to gather by the muezzin; once he himself called from the top of the minaret, now he is aided by loudspeakers. Traditionally the prayer areas in the mosques are forbidden to non-Muslims. When access is permitted you must always remove your shoes before crossing the threshold. This springs from the need to avoid dirtying the carpets that cover the floors, but in time has become merely a ritual form of respect towards the holy place.*

64 *The prohibition of alcohol is dictated by a religious precept but in Morocco this rule has been left to the free choice of the individual and not, as occurs in other Islamic countries, turned into law. Certain parts of the country produce much-appreciated wines, officially destined for non-Muslims only. Although alcohol and bars are not a part of local customs, water is very important; it was traditionally offered on the streets by street sellers dressed in bright red with wide-brimmed hats decorated with pom-poms and bells. This usage has survived in various places, Casablanca included, where the houses certainly do not lack running water. Thanks to the tinkling bells anyone in the street who feels thirsty knows where the water-seller and his "itinerant" bar is to be found.*

65 *Tea is most common drink in Morocco, as indeed in all Arab countries; this is usually flavoured with the addition of fragrant herbs and varies according to the area; mint is very popular. The preparation of this drink often takes on a ritual form, especially among the sub-Sahara populations; it is always served three times, first strong and bitter, then medium-strong, lastly weak and very sweet. In the towns the water-sellers are often joined by tea-sellers, such as the man seen in the photograph ostentatiously carrying the tea-pot on his head. Coffee is less popular despite being an Arab invention: espresso coffee can be found in hotels but elsewhere, at best, you will find Turkish coffee, made by putting toasted powder and sugar into the coffee pot.*

Berbers first and foremost

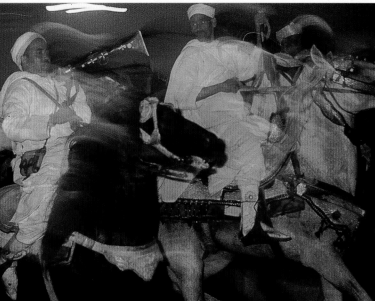

66 top *During the characteristic Berber and Arab celebrations, frenzied gallops on horseback, warrior-style, mark the major occasions such as Ras as-Sana (the lunar new year), Mouloud (Mohammed's birth), Eid Es-Sagheer (end of Ramadan, the month of fasting), and Eid el-Kabeer (the grand feast in memory of Ibrahim's sacrifice). It consists of a heady gallop of horsemen-acrobats, armed with* moukalla *(arquebuses) and dressed in traditional costume on a round track at the edge of the village; all the other members of the tribe gather around this sort of arena while the women mark the most daring manoeuvres with characteristic two-tone cries of encouragement.*

66 bottom *When the gallop comes to a climax the horses are launched towards the spectators at a fast charge which stops suddenly only in the last few yards. As the riders halt, they all fire their rifles in the air. This is all that survives of an ancient rite perhaps that may have been linked to the passage from adolescence to adulthood, at which time a test of courage was required. The use of the horse also has ancient roots in the Maghreb; the Numidian cavalry was feared in the times of the Punic wars and Berber horses are a highly valued breed, known the world over.*

66-67 *Where there is much tourism, Marrakesh for instance, this Berber tradition has lost all its original ritual meaning and become pure spectacle, staged by professional riders-acrobats. Nonetheless, it is of great effect and draws crowds of spectators.*

68 Kinship, family ties and clans play an important role in Berber society. Consequently marriage is a major collective event that will affect not only the life of the couple but often the internal balance of a ksar (village). A marriage ceremony, like this one at Merzouga, in Tafilalet, becomes a celebration for the whole community, with dancing and banquets that sometimes go on for days. On occasions such as this you may witness the guedra, an ancient ritual dance in which a woman dressed in black brings the onlookers in progressive rhythmic movements to a sort of trance. Of pre-Islamic origin, this dance has always been frowned upon by the strictest Muslims, but despite this it has survived in the customs of the Berbers of southern Morocco. Another custom unusual for an Islamic country is the moussem; held every year at Imilchil, on the High Atlas, it draws thousands of young people, male and female: a sort of "catwalk" for those seeking a partner.

69 The woman has an important place in Berber society: a form of matriarchy exists in some ethnic groups. The dress of this young woman from Merzouga should not deceive, as it suggests that she is a sort of prisoner. In actual fact the full mask that covers her face is simply the traditional bridal head-dress, like the white wedding dress worn in Europe. A woman rarely chooses her future husband, however, as marriages are usually arranged by the families.

70 top *Morocco is a good producer of cereals, cultivating wheat, barley, maize, rice and rye. Much of the barley (1 million tonnes per year) and the wheat (1.6 million tonnes) come from the Berber areas, where traditional farming methods are still in use.*

70 bottom *Mainly farmers and herdsmen, the Berbers manage to exploit even the mountainous areas for agriculture, as shown by these men busy threshing on the High Atlas.*

71 top *The Berbers also have fertile fields near Ouarzazate, on the side of the High Atlas that overlooks the Sahara. Although close to the desert, at Ouarzazate water is plentiful.*

71 bottom *The Ourika valley, just above Marrakesh, is another place where the Berbers have tilled the soil for centuries. In recent decades the inhabitants of the valley have diminished in number as the city offers better-paid jobs.*

72 top *The Moroccan tourist boom has favoured traders of carpets, like this one at Merzouga. Berber carpets are the only ones of true Moroccan origin: geometric motifs woven in goat or camel hair, often coarse to the touch, can be immediately distinguished from those "of the city", which are more elegant and refined but based on imported designs and techniques.*

72 bottom *Feared, legendary or scorned with no half measures, the "blue people" of Southern Morocco have seen their fame revived thanks to the film "The Sheltering Sky" by Bernardo Bertolucci, taken from the novel of the same title by Paul Bowles. Commonly considered Tuaregs, these men are actually Berbers of the r'guibat ethnic group; the Tuaregs live closer to the inner desert regions, spread over Algeria, Mali, Niger and Libya.*

73 *Among the "blue people" it is the men, not the women who wear a veil (tagilmus), unlike the tradition among the Arabs and most of the other Berbers. Here this custom stems not from religious canons but practical reasons: the face is covered to protect it from the sun, wind and sand.*
To guarantee this, the "blue men" use veils up to 24 feet in length and only expert hands manage to wind it around the head with the right folds, in a special way. Like their Tuareg "cousins" the blue people of Morocco have for centuries controlled transport along the caravan routes, defying the unbearable climate of the desert.

Sultans and cities

74 top *Skyscrapers, traffic, the frenetic pace of a European metropolis: with its two million inhabitants, Casablanca is the largest city in Morocco and the third largest in North Africa. The home of commerce and industry, it is the symbol of modern, prosperous Morocco. Yet this city has a troubled history: founded in the 12th century, destroyed by the Portuguese in 1468 and then by an earthquake in 1755, it has been completely rebuilt over the last two centuries.*

74 bottom *Columns flaked by time and dismantled by man: this is Volubilis, the ancient Moorish-Roman town near modern Méknès, and the symbol of Morocco's ancient history. Founded in 25 B.C., the capital of King Juba II of Mauritania, the town was conquered in A.D. 44 by the Romans; it reached its maximum splendour under the Emperor Caracalla (A.D. 188-217) before declining and being abandoned.*

75 *The entrance to the royal palace can be considered the symbol of Rabat, the sixth largest city for number of inhabitants in the country and today's capital. A fortified monastery since the 10th century and later a pirate base, Rabat has been a royal residence only since 1913.*

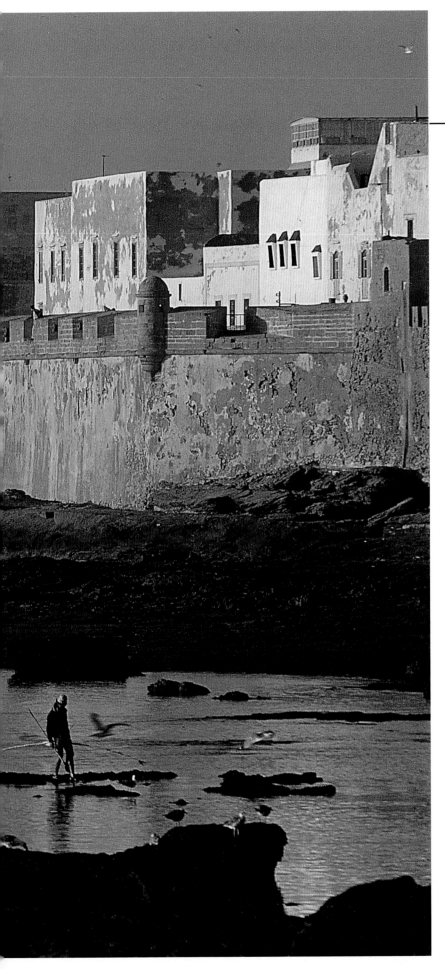

Atlantic
horizons

76-77 *The most picturesque town on the Atlantic coast is Essaouira: of ancient origin, perhaps founded by the Phoenicians, the town acquired importance thanks to the fishing of murex, molluscs from which was extracted a red dye used to colour fabric. Formerly known as Mogador, in the 16th century it was a Portuguese military base. The Portuguese built its massive walls on the ocean.*

They give it a characteristic appearance and have provided the ideal setting for historical films, including "Othello" with Orson Wells. Ever in competition with Agadir, Essaouira has in recent years become the object of a select, discreet tourism.

77 *The skalas of Essaouira are military platforms, armed with cannons and used by the Portuguese to control the port and the sea before it from the town. Two have survived intact to the present day, complete with cannon batteries.*

78-79 Just as Essaouira is picturesque, ancient and exclusive, so Agadir - its eternal rival on the Atlantic - is modern, functional and crowded. Extending along the banks of a river, Oued Sous, in a fertile region rich in vegetable gardens, Agadir was also a Portuguese base, but for a short time (1505-1541); today it is the largest seaside resort in Morocco, a symbol of successful tourism, with the best hotel amenities in the country after Marrakesh. Its fault, compared with Essaouira, is an excessive modernity making it a little cold. The present appearance of the city is not however the fruit of a specific choice: the medinas and historical monuments were destroyed by a disastrous earthquake which on 29 February 1960 shook the coast for 15 seconds. The consequences were tremendous: 15,000 dead, 20,000 homeless and 80 per cent of the buildings destroyed or seriously damaged. The Agadir of today is the result of the reconstruction worked over the last few decades.

80-81 *Modern buildings all white in colour; wide avenues that fill with cars at peak hours; a fountain that gushes intermittently, controlled by automatic timers, and every evening the star of a spectacle of light and sound: Place Mohammed V, the main crossroads in the centre of Casablanca, is the symbolic core of Morocco's most modern and efficient city. Yet, just outside the square, on the west side lies the medina (the old quarter) where the urban layout returns to the tradition of nearly all the Moroccan town centres: narrow streets arranged like a spider's web and where it is almost impossible for a car to pass because here the highway code is just one point of view and the one-way streets system is maddening. On the east side of the square is the fish and fruit market, one of the largest in the country; here the pace of the metropolis yields to tradition: despite the European appearance of the surrounding buildings, bargaining is the rule here too.*

81 *Modern buildings dominate nearly the whole of Casablanca: the three pictures are taken from different angles but show the same panorama, not so different from that of a European city. That "Casa" is an exception compared with the rest of Morocco can be seen in the numbers: 60% of the country's industries are based in this city; alone it consumes 30% of the national electrical energy although less than 5% of the population lives within its urban limits; 90% of the banks working in Morocco have their headquarters in the vicinity of Place Mohammed V. Those who remember the city of shadows and exotic atmosphere in the famous film starring Humphrey Bogart should look again: much time has passed since that film was made, and it shows.*

82-83 *Casablanca is not just modern and anonymous buildings. The colonial era left the elegant constructions of the Twenties, most to be seen around the Place des Nations Unies: they include the Palais de Justice (the law court) set amidst gardens and date palms.*

84 top left *Only opened in 1993, it is already the monument-symbol of Casablanca. The Hassan II Mosque is the largest in Morocco and indeed in all North Africa: it covers an area of almost 5 acres and can accommodate 25,000 followers inside, plus another 80,000 outside. It has the highest minaret in the world: 656 feet. 3,300 craftsmen and 35,000 labourers built it; 173,000 square feet of wood and 220,000 of plaster were carved to decorate the naves. The work was financed with a sum in excess of 300 million pounds. This gigantic mosque was built at the wish of the present king, to remember his reign in the future: for this reason it bears his name. The monument was designed to inspire marvel: electric motors can open the roof in an instant and at night a laser ray pointing from the minaret towards Mecca is visible at a distance of more than twenty miles.*

84 top right *Although it was built using the latest techniques, the design of the Hassan II Mosque was inspired by the most traditional motifs of Islamic Maghrebian architecture: porches, arches and decorations echo those of the Kairouyine Mosque in Fez. The outline of the minaret also comes from tradition: apart from the multicoloured arabesques, it resembles that of Koutoubia, the famous tower of Marrakesh.*

84 bottom *The Koran says that the throne of Allah "rests on the water" so the Hassan II Mosque was designed to stand on the waves of the Atlantic. Before construction commenced, a huge foundation pile in reinforced concrete had to be cast, and the structure was then erected on this. The final effect is remarkable: for those looking towards Casablanca from the sea the Mosque seems to rise directly from the water.*

85 top *The walls of the Hassan II Mosque are broken by frequent glass windows (to the fore of the photograph); these assure the illumination of the huge prayer area. Mainly Italian craftsmen were called upon for the glass installations of the monument. Fifty Murano glass chandeliers hang in the prayer area, where access to non-Muslims is forbidden.*

85 bottom *This view of the Hassan II Mosque highlights yet again the bond with traditional architecture. The lines of the arches on the facade as well as the majolica in the foreground are recurrent in Maghrebian and Hispano-Moorish architecture. Note the dominance of blue in the decorations: a clear reference to the sea which frames the Mosque.*

Rabat -
and the court
of the last sultan

86 left *Every country has its "father-figure": Morocco has Mohammed V, the symbol of the fight for independence and the first king after the colonial era. The neo-Moorish mausoleum in the centre of Rabat, seen here in the photograph, was dedicated to him; inside is a sarcophagus inspired by that of Napoleon, always guarded by soldiers in ceremonial uniform. Mohammed, the heir to the Alawite dynasty, reigned formally in the fifties even though Morocco was actually a French colony. In 1953 the Sultan tried to assert his true sovereignty but was immediately exiled to Corsica and replaced. A brief but violent guerilla war followed before France acknowledged independence (1955) and Mohammed returned to the throne (1957). He died a few years later leaving the throne to his eldest son, Hassan II, the present King.*

86 top right *The Museum of Moroccan Arts in Rabat is housed in a building constructed in 1680 as the local residence of Moulay Ismail, the Sultan of Méknès.*

86 bottom right *The gardens of the fortress of Rabat - the Kasbah des Oudayas - are known as the "Andalusian gardens"; this is because a large band of pirates, Muslim refugees from Spain, settled here after the Christian "reconquest" and were known as the "Andalusians".*

87 *The Tour Hassan is the most important landmark in Rabat: it was intended to be the minaret of a gigantic mosque (the second-largest in the world after that of Mecca) that Yacoub el Mansour, of the Almohad dynasty, began to construct between 1195 and 1199. It was to have 21 naves supported on 354 columns and pillars and would contain the sultan's entire army at prayer. The work remained unfinished and was then seriously damaged by the earthquake in 1755. Apart from the tower - 120 feet high and 16 each side - all that remain are 200 columns.*

88-89 *The medina of Rabat seen from Salé: the Moroccan capital lies on the left bank of the Oued Bou Regreg estuary. The oldest part, comprising the medina and the Kasbah des Oudayas, climbs up a hill. Salé, the twin town of Rabat, stands just across the river.*

89 left *A royal guard in his traditional uniform on sentry-duty in front of the Rabat palace. The sons of some families of humble origin have a hereditary right to join the guards, a corps set up in the 17th century by the Sultan Moulay Ismail, who chose his defenders from the lowest classes of the population. As well as the royal palaces, they guard Mohammed V's Mausoleum; on Friday mornings they parade on the Méchouar, the internal parade ground in the palace of Rabat.*

89 top right *The exterior of the Royal Palace, seen from the Méchouar; by day the parade ground is open to the public but by night the external gates are bolted.*

89 centre right *Elegant, well-kept, flanked by rows of date palms, Avenue Mohammed V is one of the main thoroughfares in the centre of Rabat.*

89 bottom right *The Ahl el-Fas Mosque in Rabat is where the King usually prays: it stands right opposite the palace, a hundred yards from the main entrance. On Fridays, the Muslim holy day, the king traditionally covers those hundred yards on foot, passing through cheering crowds and curious onlookers.*

90-91 *Rabat is a fascinating city, especially by night when the lights of the medina are reflected in the river.*

On the Pillars of Hercules

92-93 *Asilah, a pleasant town on the Atlantic coast, is completely surrounded by walls built by the Portuguese, who had made it their base. Behind the battlements lies a clean, tidy town, many houses being decorated with murals. There is little of Morocco at Asilah: it is more like an Andalusian or Portuguese town, as indeed it is. It has a place in the history of Morocco only because, at the beginning of this century, its governor was a pasha of proverbial despotism: Ahmed el Raisuni.*

93 top *The Pasha el Raisuni had a palace built right on the ancient Portuguese walls. Today the building is the venue for a major annual culture festival.*

93 top centre *The medina of Asilah is one of the best-kept in Morocco. The characteristic house-fronts bring to mind the fishermen's villages on the other side of the Strait of Gibraltar.*

93 bottom centre *The el Raisuni palace looms up over the small Asilah beach. It is said that before being appointed as pasha the "monster of Asilah" was a petty bandit.*

93 bottom *From the battlements of the medina of Asilah the eyes span a stretch of the Atlantic coast, at this point jagged and marked by low emerging rocks.*

94-95 *Overlooking the Atlantic on the Moroccan side of the Strait of Gibraltar, Tangier is the most European Moroccan city - in language (a strange blend of Arabic and Spanish), in custom and in culture; this is because dozens of writers and painters have come here for inspiration and Tangier has become a part of our collective imagination. One of the symbols of the city's international soul is the square in front of the central station, a funnel where the European rail network links up with that of North Africa.*

95 top *Boulevard Pasteur is the most elegant and lively street in Tangier, full of cafés, meeting places, night clubs and hotels. Here Europe is truly to hand and not just in words: at the end of the road there is a panoramic spot, Mirador de Perdicaris, from where the coast of Spain can be seen.*

95 top centre *Tangier has two markets, called Grand and Petit Socco (from the Arabic* souq*). The latter, stretched out where the medina descends towards the port, is the most fascinating with its obscure alleyways and literary memories. These were the haunts of Samuel Beckett, Tennessee Williams and Truman Capote, and today you may bump into Paul Bowles, who has decided to make his home in Tangier.*

95 bottom centre *The port of Tangier is one of the oldest in the world: it dates from the times of the Phoenicians. Today to many it represents the gate to Morocco: this is where the ferries from Europe dock, bringing thousands of tourists every year.*

95 bottom *Tangier is an extremely lively cultural centre, full of museums, clubs and institutes. The Museum of Moroccan Art, one of the most important in the city, is housed in a former royal palace.*

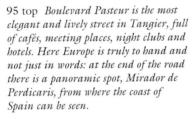

96 *Chaouen (also known as Chechaouen) is a picturesque town on the Rif, lying below mount Tisouka (6,724 feet) about forty miles from the sea. Founded in the 15th century and mainly inhabited by Muslims and Jewish refugees from Spain, it is a lovely and typical northern Moroccan provincial town. Little visited by tourists, it deserves more attention, at least on the part of linguists: its dialect is a strange old Spanish "frozen" for five centuries.*

97 top *The kasbah of Chaouen, rising in the centre of the medina, is reminiscent of the era of Abd el Krim, an anti-colonial rebel, hastily classed as a "bandit" by the Europeans. At the turn of the century he kept the French and Spanish colonial troops at bay with a rebellion that lasted years. In his defensive position on the Rif, clearly supported by the local Berber people, the "bandit" seemed unassailable but was forced to give himself up in 1926 and was imprisoned here in this very kasbah.*

97 bottom *The Chaouen mosque stands on the main square; Abd el Krim, the last "bandit" of the Rif, gave himself up to the French troops here in front of this holy place in 1926. The local peoples have always been reluctant to accept any - not just colonial - external authority. So it is logical that Abd el Krim should today be remembered as a hero of the independence movement. To cushion the drive for autonomy the King allows a local radio to broadcast in dialect.*

97

98-99 The combination of white and blue prevails among the houses of the medina of Chaouen, one of the most picturesque and best-kept in all Morocco. Painting the houses white is a defence against the rays of the sun and, apparently, the blue serves to repel flies as these insects are said to have a natural aversion to this colour. Whether this entomological observation is true or not, many parts of the Mediterranean have houses painted in these colours. This is not a consistent custom in Morocco, Chaouen is an exception. The tidy simplicity of the houses and the use of colours are more reminiscent of certain parts of Andalusia or Tunisia than of the Moroccan interior.

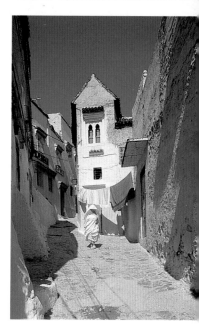

The Pompeii of the Maghreb

100 top *The arch of Caracalla rises majestically above the main thoroughfare of Volubilis, a Roman town 30 kilometres north of Méknès. Despite the name, this monument was almost certainly the work of Marcus Aurelius (A.D.121-180).*

100 bottom *At the time of Caracalla, Volubilis numbered 20,000 inhabitants. The town was demolished in part by the Sultan of Méknès in the 17th century. An earthquake in 1755 completed the work of destruction.*

101 left *Still visible in the centre of the town, slightly higher than the rest of the Forum, are the ruins of the Capitol, of which only eight columns remain. Near here archaeologists found statues still in good condition but for reasons of safety all the material has been transferred to the archaeological museum in Rabat.*

101 right *The ruins of the Basilica, the ancient meeting-place and market, are more easily interpreted. The majesty of the building confirms the commercial importance of Volubilis in the past; it flourished until the third century of the Christian era. Although the town was founded by native peoples, few traces of the pre-Roman period remain - a sign of the large-scale intervention on the part of the conquerors.*

102-103 *The most precious finds at Volubilis are the mosaics that embellish the floors of certain noblemen's residences. The best-decorated houses in the town are those of "Orpheus", "the Cortege of Venus", "the labours of Hercules", "Bacchus and the four seasons", "the Nymphs bathing". All these names refer to the subjects of the mosaics, dating from the 2nd and 3rd centuries A.D. The mosaic known as the "Cortege of Venus" is highly refined - as shown in the picture - and potrays the naked goddess bathing between two nymphs.*

103 top *Beside the "House of Bacchus and the four seasons", towards the Forum of Volubilis, lie the remains of a house with a large mosaic floor depicting the mythical "seven labours" of Hercules.*

103 bottom *Inside the "House of Bacchus and the four seasons" is a famous mosaic dedicated to the Roman god of wine, crowned with vine shoots and leaves. The image is important because it proves the propagation of the Dyonisian cults were bound to vine growing and wine producing activities, and at the time, these had clearly spread to the most south-western parts of the Empire. It is curious to note that wine is still produced at Méknès, not far from here.*

Fez, the ancient core of Morocco

104 top *Fez was founded by Sultan Moulay Idriss II in 808 but it was made great by the Merinids, who ruled here for three hundred years, starting in 1250. The great tombs, the ruins of which can be seen outside the gates, were erected for this family.*

104 bottom *Fez has two old centres, Fez Jdid and Fez el Bali, very different from each other and each encircled by walls; those of Fez Jdid, dating from the 14th century, also encompass the Royal Palace.*

105 top *Fez el Bali grew under the Idrissids in the 9th century. The oldest quarter of the city is still an intricate maze of streets and alleyways; above these rise the minarets of the mosques and* medersa, *the Koranic schools for which Fez is famous throughout the Muslim world.*

105 bottom *The most famous monument in Fez el Bali is the Kairouyine Mosque, the largest in Morocco before the recent construction of that in Casablanca. Founded in 859, it was restructured in the 12th century. Annexed to the mosque is the university of the same name, the oldest in the world.*

106-107 *The ancient core of Fez is enclosed within a circle of walls; seen from the outside it seems a single, blurred expanse of houses, all the same and painted in light colours.*

108-109 *At the centre of the Merinid quarter of Fez Jdid stands the Royal Palace where King Hassan II sometimes resides. Like that of Rabat, this secondary palace is closed to the public, except for the square in front of it. The adjacent royal gardens, said to be the loveliest in Morocco, are also off limits to visitors. It is curious that the Royal Palace stands close to the* mellah, *the Jewish quarter. Today there are few Jews in Fez but there used to be a flourishing community, the most important religious minority in the city.*

109 top *Eight* bab *or gates open in the walls of Fez el Bali. The most famous and impressive is Bab Boujeloud leading to Rue du Grand Talaa, the main access route to the medina. Just through the gate - tiled with majolica - towers the minaret of Medersa Bou Inania, one of the most characteristic in Fez.*

109 bottom *More austere than Bab Boujeloud are the entrances in the walls of Fez Jdid, dating from the Merinid era (14th century). The colour of the monuments in Fez is always the same whatever era or quarter they belong to. For this unique feature Fez Jdid and Fez el Bali have been included by UNESCO in the "World Heritage Sites".*

110 top *Thanks to clever effects of artificial lights, by night Bab Boujeloud becomes even more attractive and visions of the sumptuous processions of the Merinid era are conjured up before its three arches. Appearances must not deceive: Bab Boujeloud was built in 1913.*

110 bottom *A mausoleum in the heart of Fez el Bali is dedicated to Moulay Idriss II, the sultan who founded Fez. Repeatedly retouched, richly decorated and covered with green tiles, the present version of this monument dates from the 18th century.*

111 *In tribute to the precepts of the Koran which call for reserve among the wealthy, the exterior of the houses and palaces of Fez are usually not very ostentatious. The abundance of decoration, stucco-work and majolica is all kept for the interiors: this is so for the Mehnebi palace in Fez el Bali.*

112 *The Kasbah des Cherarda, a 17th century fortress on a scenic rise, stands beside Fez Jdid.*
The artificial lights that are lit every evening accentuate its powerful structure. See how many people fill the streets of Fez by night: as all the Moroccan towns, the "moral capital" dozes in the middle of the day (extremely hot in summer) and revives when the sun sets and the air is cooler.

113 top *The walls of Fez Jdid, here seen by night, were restored recently, partly thanks to a contribution from UNESCO. The two districts of Fez el Bali and Fez Jdid together form the largest medina in Morocco and are home to 300,000 people. Maintenance of the buildings is very expensive and not always satisfactory; just outside these well-kept walls is the* mellah, *the Jewish quarter, with its tumbledown houses.*

113 bottom *The Bou Inania Medrasa - the Koranic school - is the most important and finest in Fez. It was built between 1350 and 1357 by Sultan Abou Inan who wanted to compete with the university of the Kairouyine Mosque, even then famous all over North Africa. The Sultan spared no expense increasing the prestige of his creation: it was decorated with sculptures, the ablution baths were filled from a deviation of the river that crosses the city, Oued Fez, and when work was completed - so a legend tells - he had the accounts books for the works thrown into the Oued, as a sign that art has no price.*

Méknès, sombre but grandiose

114 top *The Mausoleum of Moulay Ismail is still the busiest place in Méknès. Although he has always been classed in Europe as a tyrant, in his towns Ismail is revered as a saint or a hero. Inside, the mausoleum reflects this cult: it is monumental and richly decorated.*

114 top centre *From the outside, the Royal Palace is of sober design, in line with the recommendations of the Koran which condemns the ostentation of wealth. Only its great doors are magnificently decorated with polychrome majolica tiles.*

114 bottom centre *Beneath the citadel of Méknès are huge granaries, their vaulted ceilings creating strange echoes. The fortress of Moulay Ismail was designed to withstand prolonged sieges; ample store-houses were therefore required for the accumulation of the huge quantities of provisions necessary for the forces of the garrison which numbered 30,000 soldiers.*

114 bottom *Today's Royal Palace, inside the citadel of Moulay Ismail, is nothing like the original one, destroyed shortly after the Sultan's death. This royal palace, closed to the public, is one of the King's secondary residences.*

114-115 *Elegant courtyards open in the Moulay Ismail Mausoleum, conceived according to the canons of Moorish architecture but embellished with European features, such as the Corinthian capitals seen in the photograph. The sarcophagus of the Sultan lies in a room that can be admired only from outside; it is adorned with two pendulum clocks, "wonders" donated to Ismail by Louis XIV of France, the "Sun King".*

116-117 *The only monument in Méknès not bound to the memory of Moulay Ismail is the Medrassa Bou Inania; this Koranic school - like that of the same name in Fez - was built by Sultan Abou Inan around 1350. Here too, just like at Fez, the Sultan had the walls decorated with stucco-work and arabesques in plenty.*

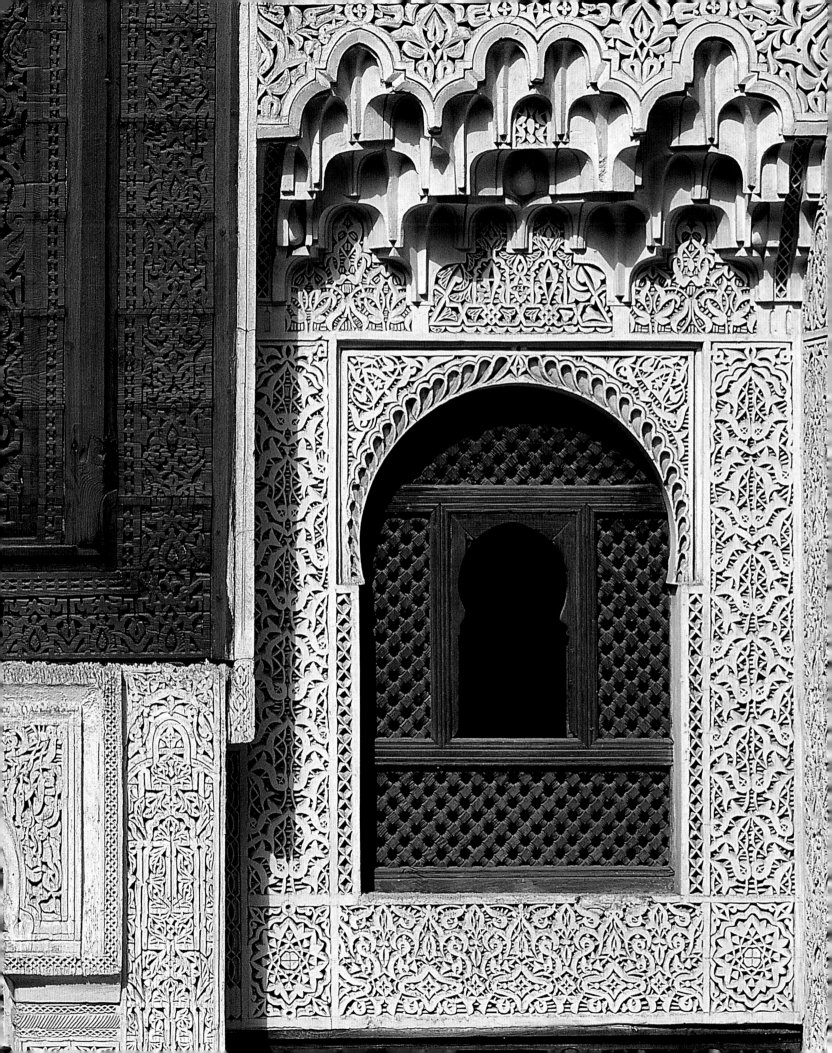

Marrakesh, the best-loved city

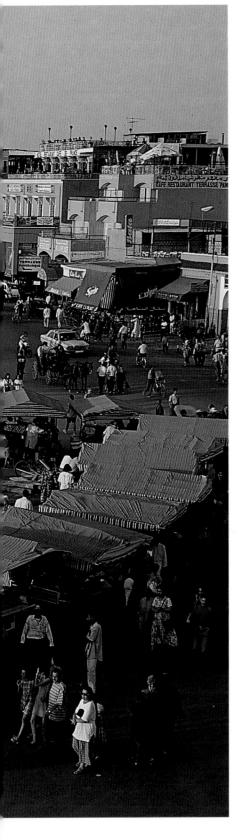

118-119 *Although not surrounded by important monuments, Djemma el Fna is the most famous square in Morocco. It stands in the centre of the city, a short distance from the entrance to the* souq, *the huge market of the medina; at all times of the day and night it is alive with a multicoloured and changing crowd: street-sellers, jugglers, story-tellers, snake-charmers. Despite today's liveliness, the origin of the square was anything but cheerful: Djemma el Fna means "meeting place of the hanged" because this is where executions were held.*

119 top *Bab Aghmat may not be the loveliest but it is certainly the most important of the gates in the walls of Marrakesh: a monument rich in symbolic meaning and historical references. This is where the ancient trail that climbed the High Atlas to Ouarzazate and the Sahara started. For centuries this gate marked the imaginary boundary between the Morocco of the Imperial cities and the pre-desert areas of the south. And from the south came the founder of this city, Sultan Youssef ibn Tashfin (1070-1107), of the Almoravid dynasty.*

119 bottom *Sixty-two sultans and court notables, with their respective wives and children, are buried in the Saadian tombs, an enormous mausoleum built for Ahmed el Mansour (1578-1603), the "Lawrence the Magnificent of Marrakesh". The tombs are distributed in three pavilions, covered with ceilings in cedarwood and supported on columns of Carrara marble. The internal walls are filled with inscriptions from various eras: a veritable text book on the evolution of Arab handwriting.*

120-121 *Even by night Djemma el Fna bustles with life, especially during Ramadan, the lunar month of fasting when practising Muslims abstain from food and drink between dawn and dusk and then once the sun has set dine ritually in company. The large square in Marrakesh thus becomes the main place of evening encounter: the stalls offer couscous, chicken with lemon, rice, mint tea and the traditional sweetmeats only eaten at this time of the year.*

123 top left *The Bahia Palace is often used as a set for films with an oriental flavour: years ago some scenes of the film "The Lion and the Wind" were filmed in this courtyard.*

123 bottom left *Fountains are a recurrent note in the Bahia Palace: a true status-symbol in a country where water is a precious asset...*

123 top right *Inside the Bahia Palace are lush gardens, as in the other old palaces of the city. The best-known garden in Marrakesh is however the Menara.*

123 bottom right *When not occupied by the king's visitors the Bahia Palace is open to the public as a normal museum. Inside you can admire the splendid rooms adorned with the finest of majolicas.*

124 *In Marrakesh, as in all the imperial cities, the King has a royal palace that serves as a secondary residence. But here Hassan II's stays are not merely occasional and symbolic: the sovereign spends three months of the year in the former capital of the Almoravid dynasty. The Royal Palace of Marrakesh is of recent origin; it was built at the beginning of this century by the powerful local el Glaoui family and only at a later stage yielded to the royal family.*

125 top *A mighty rampart, refined by flower and shell decorations: Bab Agnaou, the most elegant and spectacular gate of Marrakesh. Made so by the Almoravid Sultan Yacoub el Mansour (1184-1199), not to be confused with the 16th-century Ahmed el Mansour). Bab Agnaou was part of a huge kasbah, formed of twelve palaces and surrounded by defensive lakes. The* kasbah *has almost totally been destroyed.*

125 bottom *Said to be the oldest gate in Marrakesh: it certainly looks it judging by the austere, square towers, in keeping with the original spirit of the city; before becoming the lively and cheerful metropolis of today it was the stronghold of the Almoravids, warriors and integralists. The gate is called Bab el Rahna; often fake "blue people" are to be seen hanging around near it with their camels. They are nothing to do with Marrakesh, only there asking for money to pose for the tourists' cameras. This too is Morocco today.*